THE MISSION OF MR. EUSTACE GREYNE

Robert Hichens

[ZHINGOORA BOOKS]

This edition is published by
Zhingoora Books.

Contents

I

Mrs. Eustace Greyne (pronounced Green) wrinkled her forehead—that noble, that startling forehead which had been written about in the newspapers of two hemispheres—laid down her American Squeezer pen, and sighed. It was an autumn day, nipping and melancholy, full of the rustle of dying leaves and the faint sound of muffin bells, and Belgrave Square looked sad even to the great female novelist who had written her way into a mansion there. Fog hung about with the policeman on the pavement. The passing motor cars were like shadows. Their stertorous pantings sounded to Mrs. Greyne's ears like the asthma of dying monsters. She sighed again, and murmured in a deep contralto voice: "It must be so." Then she got up, crossed the heavy Persian carpet which had been bought with the proceeds of a short story in her earlier days, and placed her forefinger upon an electric bell.

Like lightning a powdered giant came.

"Has Mr. Greyne gone out?"

"No, ma'am."

"Where is he?"

"In his study, ma'am, pasting the last of the cuttings into the new album."

Mrs. Greyne smiled. It was a pretty picture the unconscious six-footer had conjured up.

"I am sorry to disturb Mr. Greyne," she answered, with that gracious, and even curling suavity which won all hearts; "but I wish to see him. Will you ask him to come to me for a moment?"

The giant flew, silk-stockinged, to obey the mandate, while Mrs. Greyne sat down on a carved oaken chair of ecclesiastical aspect to await her husband.

She was a famous woman, a personage, this simply-attired lady. With an American Squeezer pen she had won fame, fortune, and a mansion in Belgrave Square, and all without the sacrifice of principle. Respectability incarnate, she had so dealt with the sorrows and evils of the world that she had rendered them utterly acceptable to Mrs. Grundy, Mr. Grundy, and all the Misses Grundy. People said she dived into the depths of human nature, and brought up nothing that need scandalise a curate's grandmother, or the whole-aunt of an archdeacon; and this was so true that she had made a really prodigious amount of money. Her large, her solid, her unrelenting books lay upon every table. Even the smart set kept them, uncut—like pretty sinners who have never been "found out"—to give an air of haphazard intellectuality to frisky boudoirs, All the clergy, however unable to get their tithes, bought them. All bishops alluded to them in "pulpit utterances." Fabulous prices were paid for them by magazine editors. They ran as serials through all the tale of months. The suburbs battened on them. The provinces adored them. Country people talked of no other literature. In fact, Mrs. Eustace Greyne was a really fabulous success.

Why, then, should she heave these heavy sighs in Belgrave Square? Why should she lift an intellectual hand as though to tousle the glossy chestnut bandeaux which swept back from her forcible forehead, and screw her reassuring features into these wrinkles of perplexity and distress?

The door opened, and Mr. Eustace Greyne appeared, "What is it, Eugenia?" upon his lips.

Mr. Greyne was a number of years younger than his celebrated wife, and looked even younger than his years. He was a very smart man, with smooth, jet-black hair, which he wore parted in the middle; pleasant, dark eyes that could twinkle gently; a clear, pale complexion; and a nice, tall figure. One felt, in glancing at him, that he had been an Eton boy, and had at least thought of going into the militia at some period of his life. His history can be briefly told.

Scarcely had he emerged into the world before he met and was married to Mrs. Eustace Greyne, then Miss Eugenia Hannibal-Barker. He had had no time to sow a single oat, wild or otherwise; no time to adore a barmaid, or wish to have his name linked with that of an actress; no time to do anything wrong, or even to know, with the complete accuracy desired by all persevering young men, what was really wrong. Miss Eugenia Hannibal-Barker sailed upon his horizon, and he struck his flag to matrimony. Ever since then he had been her husband, and had never, even for one second, emerged beyond the boundaries of the most intellectual respectability. He was the most innocent of men, although he knew all the important editors in London. Swaddled in money by his successful wife, he considered her a goddess. She poured the thousands into Coutts' Bank, and with the arrival of each fresh thousand he was more firmly convinced that she was a goddess. To say he looked up to her would be too mild. As the Cockney tourist in Chamounix peers at the summit of Mont Blanc, he peered at Mrs. Greyne. And when, finally, she bought the lease of the mansion in Belgrave Square, he knew her Delphic.

So now he appeared in the oracle's retreat respectfully, "What is it, Eugenia?" upon his admiring lips.

"Sit down, my husband," she murmured.

Mr. Greyne subsided by the fire, placing his pointed patent-leather toes upon the burnished fender. Without the fog grew deeper, and the chorus of the muffin bells more plaintive. The fire-light, flickering over Mrs. Greyne's majestic features, made them look Rembrandtesque. Her large, oxlike eyes were fixed and thoughtful. After a pause, she said:

"Eustace, I shall have to send you upon a mission."

"A mission, Eugenia!" said Mr. Greyne in great surprise.

"A mission of the utmost importance, the utmost delicacy."

"Has it anything to do with Romeike & Curtice?"

"No."

"Will it take me far?"

"That is my trouble. It will take you very far."

"Out of London?"

"Oh, yes."

"Out of—not out of England?"

"Yes; it will take you to Algeria."

"Good gracious!" cried Mr. Greyne.

Mrs. Greyne sighed.

"Good gracious!" Mr. Greyne repeated after a short interval. "Am I to go alone?" "Of course you must take Darrell." Darrell was Mr. Greyne's valet.

"And what am I to do at Algiers?"

"You must obtain for me there the whole of the material for book six of 'Catherine's Repentance,'" "Catherine's Repentance" was the gigantic novel upon which Mrs. Greyne was at that moment engaged.

"I will not disguise from you, Eustace," continued Mrs. Greyne, looking increasingly Rembrandtesque, "that, in my present work, I am taking a somewhat new departure."

"Well, but we are very comfortable here," said Mr. Greyne.

With each new book they had changed their abode. "Harriet" took them from Phillimore Gardens to Queensgate Terrace; "Jane's Desire" moved them on to a corner house in Sloane Street; with "Isobel's Fortune" they passed to Curzon Street; "Susan's Vanity" landed them in Coburg Place; and, finally, "Margaret's Involution" had planted them in Belgrave Square. Now, with each of these works of genius Mrs. Greyne had taken what she called "a new departure." Mr. Greyne's remark is, therefore, explicable.

"True. Still, there is always Park Lane."

She mused for a moment. Then, leaning more heavily upon the carved lions of her chair, she continued:

"Hitherto, although I have sometimes dealt with human frailty, I have treated it gently. I have never betrayed a Zola-spirit."

"Zola! My darling!" cried Mr. Eustace Greyne. "You are surely not going to betray anything of that sort now!"

"If she does we shall soon have to move off to West Kensington," was his secret thought.

"No. But in book six of 'Catherine' I have to deal with sin, with tumult, with African frailty. It is inevitable."

She sighed once more. The burden of the new book was very heavy upon her.

"African frailty!" murmured the astonished Eustace Greyne.

"Now, neither you nor I, my husband, know anything about this."

"Certainly not, my darling. How should we? We have never explored beyond Lucerne."

"We must, therefore, get to know about it—at least you must. For I cannot leave London. The continuity of the brain's travelling must not be imperiled by any violent bodily activity. In the present stage of my book a sea journey might be disastrous."

"Certainly you should keep quiet, my love. But then——"

"You must go for me to Algiers. There you must get me what I want. I fear you will have to poke about in the native quarters a good deal for it, so you had better buy two revolvers, one for yourself and one for Darrell."

Mr. Greyne gasped. The calmness of his wife amazed him. He was not intellectual enough to comprehend fully the deep imaginings of a mighty brain, the obsession work is in the worker.

"African frailty is what I want," pursued Mrs. Greyne. "One hundred closely-printed pages of African frailty. You will collect for me the raw material, and I shall so manipulate it that it will fall discreetly, even elevatingly, into the artistic whole. Do you understand me, Eustace?"

"I am to travel to Algiers, and see all the wickedness to be seen there, take notes of it, and bring them back to you."

"Precisely."

"And how long am I to stay?"

"Until you have made yourself acquainted with the depths."

"A fortnight?"

"I should think that would be enough. Take Brush's remedy for seasickness and plenty of antipyrin, your fur coat for the crossing, and a white helmet and umbrella for the arrival. You have lead pencils?"

"Plenty."

"A couple of Merrin's exercise-books should be enough to contain your notes."

"When am I to go?"

"The sooner the better. I am at a standstill for want of the material. You might catch the express to Paris to-morrow; no, say the day after to-morrow." She looked at him tenderly. "The parting will be bitter."

"Very bitter," Mr. Eustace Greyne replied.

He felt really upset. Mrs. Greyne laid the hand which had brought them from Phillimore Gardens to Belgrave Square gently upon his.

"Think of the result," she said. "The greatest book I have done yet. A book that will last. A book that will——"

"Take us to Park Lane," he murmured.

The Rembrandtesque head nodded. The noble features, as of a strictly respectable Roman emperor, relaxed.

"A book that will take us to Park Lane."

At this moment the door opened, and the footman inquired:

"Could Mademoiselle Verbena see you for a minute, ma'am?"

Mademoiselle Verbena was the French governess of the two little Greynes. The great novelist had consented to become a mother.

"Certainly."

In another moment Mademoiselle Verbena was added to the group beside the fire.

II

We have said that Mademoiselle Verbena was the French governess of little Adolphus and Olivia Greyne, and so she was to this extent—that she taught them French, and that Mr. and Mrs. Greyne supposed her to be a Parisian. But life has its little ironies. Mademoiselle Verbena in the house of this great and respectable novelist was one of them; for she was a Levantine, born at Port Said of a Suez Canal father and a Suez Canal mother. Now, nobody can desire to say anything against Port Said. At the same time, few mothers would inevitably pick it out as the ideal spot from which a beneficent influence for childhood's happy hour would be certain to emanate. Nor, it must be allowed, is a Suez Canal ancestry specially necessary to a trainer of young souls. It may not be a drawback, but it can hardly be described as an advantage. This, Mademoiselle Verbena was intelligent enough to know. She, therefore, concealed the fact that her father had been a dredger of Monsieur de Lesseps' triumph, her mother a bar-lady of the historic coal wharf where the ships are fed, and preferred to suppose—and to permit others to suppose—that she had first seen the light in the Rue St. Honoré, her parents being a count and countess of some old régime.

This supposition, retained from her earliest years, had affected her appearance and her manner. She was a very neat, very trim, even a very attractive little person, with dark brown, roguish eyes, blue-black hair, a fairy-like figure, and the prettiest hands and feet imaginable. She had first attracted Mrs. Greyne's attention by her devotion to St. Paul's Cathedral, and this devotion she still kept up. Whenever she had an hour or two free she always—so she herself said—spent it in "*ce charmant* St. Paul."

As she entered the oracle's retreat she cast down her eyes, and trembled visibly.

"What is it, Miss Verbena?" inquired Mrs. Greyne, with a kindly English accent, calculated to set any poor French creature quite at ease.

Mademoiselle Verbena trembled more.

"I have received bad news, madame."

"I grieve to hear it. Of what nature?"

"Mamma has *une bronchite très grave.*"

"A what, Miss Verbena?"

"Pardon, madame. A very grave bronchitis. She cries for me."

"Indeed!"

"The doctors say she will die."

"This is very sad."

The Levantine wept. Even Suez Canal folk are not proof against all human sympathy. Mr. Greyne blew his nose beside the fire, and Mrs. Greyne said again:

"I repeat that this is very sad."

"Madame, if I do not go to mamma tomorrow I shall not see her more."

Mrs. Greyne looked very grave.

"Oh!" she remarked. She thought profoundly for a moment, and then added: "Indeed!"

"It is true, madame."

Suddenly Mademoiselle Verbena flung herself down on the Persian carpet at Mrs. Greyne's large but well-proportioned feet, and, bathing them with her tears, cried in a heartrending manner:

"Madame will let me go! madame will permit me to fly to poor mamma—to close her dying eyes—to kiss once again——"

Mr. Greyne was visibly affected, and even Mrs. Greyne seemed somewhat put about, for she moved her feet rather hastily out of reach of the dependant's emotion, and made her scramble up.

"Where is your poor mother?"

"In Paris, madame. In the Rue St. Honoré, where I was born. Oh, if she should die there! If she should——"

Mrs. Greyne raised her hand, commanding silence.

"You wish to go there?"

"If madame permits."

"When?"

"To-morrow, madame."

"To-morrow? This is decidedly abrupt."

"*Mais la bronchite, madame*, she is abrupt, and death, she may be abrupt."

"True. One moment!"

There was an instant's silence for Mrs. Greyne to let loose her brain in. She did so, then said:

"You have my permission. Go to-morrow, but return as soon as possible. I do not wish Adolphus to lose his still uncertain grasp upon the irregular verbs."

In a flood of grateful tears Mademoiselle Verbena retired to make her preparations. On the morrow she was gone.

The morrow was a day of much perplexity, much bustle and excitement for Mr. Greyne and the valet, Darrell. They were preparing for Algiers. In the morning, at an early hour, Mr. Greyne set forth in the barouche with Mrs. Greyne to purchase African necessaries: a small but well-supplied medicine chest, a pith helmet, a white-and-green umbrella, a Baedeker, a couple of Smith & Wesson Springfield revolvers with a due amount of cartridges, a dozen of Merrin's exercise-books—on mature reflection Mrs. Creyne thought that two would hardly contain a sufficient amount of African frailty for her present purpose—a packet of lead pencils, some bottles of a remedy for seasickness, a silver flask for cognac, and various other trifles such as travellers in distant continents require.

Meanwhile Darrell was learning French for the journey, and packing his own and his master's trunks. The worthy fellow, a man of twenty-five summers, had never been across the Channel—the Greynes being by no means prone to foreign travel—and it may, therefore, be imagined that he was in a state of considerable expectation as he laid the trousers, coats, and waistcoats in their respective places, selected such boots as seemed likely to wear well in a tropical climate, and dropped those shirts which are so contrived as to admit plenty of ventilation to the heated body into the case reserved for them.

When Mr. Greyne returned from his shopping excursion the barouche, loaded almost to the gunwale—if one may be permitted a nautical expression in this connection—had to be disburdened, and its contents conveyed upstairs to Mr. Greyne's bedroom, into which Mrs. Greyne herself presently entered to give directions for their disposing. Nor was it till the hour of sunset that everything was in due order, the straps set fast, the keys duly turned in the locks—the labels—"Mr. Eustace Greyne: Passenger to Algiers: via Marseilles"—carefully written out in a full, round hand. Rook's tickets had been bought; so now everything was ready, and the last evening in England might be spent by Mr. Greyne in the drawing-room and by Darrell in the servants' hall quietly, socially, perhaps pathetically.

The pathos of the situation, it must be confessed, appealed more to the master than to the servant. Darrell was very gay, and inclined to be boastful, full of information as to how he would comport himself with "them there Frenchies," and how he would make "them pore, godless Arabs sit up." But Mr. Greyne's attitude of mind was very different. As the night drew on, and Mrs. Greyne and he sat by the wood fire in the magnificent drawing-room, to which they always adjourned after dinner, a keen sense of the sorrow of departure swept over them both.

"How lonely you will feel without me, Eugenia," said Mr. Greyne. "I have been thinking of that all day."

"And you, Eustace, how desolate will be your tale of days! My mind runs much on that. You will miss me at every hour."

"You are so accustomed to have me within call, to depend upon me for encouragement in your life-work. I scarcely know how you will get on when I am far across the sea."

"And you, for whom I have labored, for whom I have planned and calculated, what will be your sensations when you realize that a gulf—the Gulf of Lyons—is fixed irrevocably between us?"

So their thoughts ran. Each one was full of tender pity for the other. Towards bedtime, however, conscious that the time for colloquy was running short, they fell into more practical discourse.

"I wonder," said Mr. Greyne, "whether I shall find any difficulty in gaining the information you require, my darling. I suppose these places"—he spoke vaguely, for his thoughts were vague—"are somewhat awkward to come at. Naturally they would avoid the eye of day."

Mrs. Greyne looked profound.

"Yes. Evil ever seeks the darkness. You will have to do the same."

"You think my investigations must take place at night?"

"I should certainly suppose so."

"And where shall I find a cicerone?"

"Apply to Rook."

"In what terms? You see, dearest, this is rather a special matter, isn't it?"

"Very special. But on no account hint that you are in Algiers for 'Catherine's' sake. It would get into the papers. It would be cabled to America. The whole reading world would be agog, and the future interest of the book discounted."

Mr. Greyne looked at his wife with reverence. In such moments he realized, almost too poignantly, her great position.

"I will be careful," he said. "What would you recommend me to say?"

"Well"—Mrs. Greyne knit her superb forehead—"I should suggest that you present yourself as an ordinary traveler, but with a specially inquiring bent of mind and a slight tendency towards the—the—er—hidden things of life."

"I suppose you wish me to visit the public houses?"

"I wish you to see everything that has part or lot in African frailty. Go everywhere, see everything. Bring your notes to me, and I will select such fragments of the broken commandments as suit my purpose, which is, as always, the edifying of the human race. Only this time I mean to purge it as by fire."

"That corner house in Park Lane, next to the Duke of Ebury's, would suit us very well," said Mr. Greyne reflectively.

"We could sell our lease here at an advance," his wife rejoined. "You will not waste your journey, Eustace?"

"My love," returned Mr. Greyne with decision, "I will apply to Rook on arrival, and, if I find his man unsatisfactory, if I have any reason to suspect that I am not being shown everything—more especially in the Kasbah region, which, from the guide-books we bought to-day, is, I take it, the most abandoned portion of the city—I will seek another cicerone."

"Do so. And now to bed. You must sleep well to-night in preparation for the journey."

It was their invariable habit before retiring to drink each a tumbler of barley water, which was set out by the butler in Mrs. Greyne's study. After this nightcap Mrs. Greyne wrote up her anticipatory diary, while Mr. Greyne smoked a mild cigar, and then they went to bed. To-night, as usual, they repaired to the sanctum, and drank their barley water. Having done so, Mr. Greyne drew forth his cigar-case, while Mrs. Greyne went to her writing-table, and prepared to unlock the drawer in which her diary reposed, safe from all prying eyes.

The match was struck, the key was inserted in the lock, and turned. As the cigar end glowed the drawer was opened. Mr. Greyne heard a contralto cry. He turned from the arm-chair in which he was just about to seat himself.

"My love, is anything the matter?"

His wife was bending forward with both hands in the drawer, telling over its contents.

"My diary is not here!"

"Your diary!"

"It is gone."

"But"—he came over to her—"this is very serious. I presume, like all diaries, it is full of——" Instinctively he had been about to say "damning"; he remembered his dear one's irreproachable character and substituted "precious secrets."

"It is full of matter which must never be given to the world—my secret thoughts, my aspirations. The whole history of my soul is there."

"Heavens! It must be found."

They searched the writing-table. They searched the room. No diary.

"Could you have taken it to my room, and left it there?" asked Mr. Greyne.

They hastened thither, and looked—in vain. By this time the servants were gone to bed, and the two searchers were quite alone on the ground floor of their magnificent mansion. Mrs. Greyne began to look seriously perturbed. Her Roman features worked.

"This is appalling," she exclaimed. "Some thief, knowing it priceless, must have stolen the diary. It will be published in America. It will bring in thousands—but to others, not to us."

She began to wring her hands. It was near midnight.

"Think, my love, think!" cried Mr. Greyne. "Where could you have taken it? You had it last night?"

"Certainly. I remember writing in it that you would be sailing to Algiers on the *Général Bertrand* on Thursday of this week, and that on the night I should be feeling widowed here. The previous night I wrote that yesterday I should have to tell you of your mission. You know I always put down beforehand what I shall do, what I shall even think on each succeeding day. It is a practice that regulates the mind and conduct, that helps to uniformity."

"How true! Who can have taken it? Do you ever leave it about?"

"Never. Am I a madwoman?"

"My darling, compose yourself! We must search the house."

They proceeded to do so, and, on coming into the schoolroom, Mrs. Greyne, who was in front, uttered a sudden cry.

Upon the table of Mademoiselle Verbena lay the diary, open at the following entry:—

On Thursday next poor Eustace will be on board the *Général Bertrand*, sailing for Algiers. I shall be here thinking of myself, and of him in relation to myself. God help us both. Duty is sometimes stern. Mem. The corner house in Park Lane, next the Duke of Ebury's, has sixty years still to run; the lease, that is. Thursday—poor Eustace!

"What does this portend?" cried Mrs. Greyne.

"My darling, it passes my wit to imagine," replied her husband.

III

The parting of Mr. and Mrs. Greyne on the following morning was very affecting. It took place at Victoria Station, in the midst of a small crowd of admiring strangers, who had recognised the commanding presence of the great novelist, and had gathered round to observe her manifestations.

Mrs. Greyne was considerably shaken by the event of the previous night. Although, on the discovery of the diary, the house had been roused, and all the servants closely questioned, no light had been thrown upon its migration from the locked drawer to the schoolroom table. Adolphus and Olivia, jerked from sleep by the hasty hands of a maid, could only weep and wan. The powdered footmen, one and all, declared they had never heard of a diary. The butler gave warning on the spot, keeping on his nightcap to give greater effect to his pronunciamento. It was all most unsatisfactory, and for one wild moment Mrs. Greyne seriously thought of retaining her husband by her as a protection against the mysterious thief who had been at work in their midst. Could it be Mademoiselle Verbena? The dread surmise occurred, but Mr. Greyne rejected it.

"Her father was a count," he said. "Besides, my darling, I don't believe she can read English; certainly not unless it is printed."

So there the matter rested, and the moment of parting came.

There was a murmur of respectful sympathy as Mrs. Greyne clasped her husband tenderly in her arms, and pressed his head against her prune-coloured bonnet strings. The whistle sounded. The train moved on. Leaning from a reserved first-class compartment, Mr. Greyne waved a silk pocket-handkerchief so long as his wife's Roman profile stood out clear against the fog and smoke of London. But at last it faded, grew remote, took on the appearance of a feebly-executed crayon drawing, vanished. He sank back upon the cushions—alone. Darrell was travelling second with the dressing-case.

It was a strange sensation, to be alone, and *en route* to Algiers. Mr. Greyne scarcely knew what to make of it. A schoolboy suddenly despatched to Timbuctoo could hardly have felt more terribly emancipated than he did. He was so absolutely unaccustomed to freedom, he had been for so long without the faintest desire for it, that to have it thrust upon him so suddenly was almost alarming. He felt lonely, anxious, horribly unmarried. To divert his thoughts he drew forth a Merrin's exercise-book and a pencil, and wrote on the first page, in large letters, "*African Frailty, Notes for*" Then he sat gazing at the title of his first literary work, and wondering what on earth he was going to see in Algiers.

Vague visions of himself in the bars of African public-houses, in mosques, in the two-pair-backs of dervishes, in bazaars—which he pictured to himself like those opened by royalties at the Queen's Hall—in Moorish interiors surrounded by voluptuous ladies with large oval eyes, black tresses, and Turkish trousers of spangled muslin, flitted before his mental gaze. When the train ran upon Dover Pier, and the white horses of the turbulent Channel foamed at his feet, he started as one roused from a Rip Van Winkle sleep. Severe illness occupied his whole attention for a time, and then recovery.

In Paris he dined at the buffet like one in a dream, and, at the appointed hour, came forth to take the *rapide* for Marseilles. He looked for Darrell and the dressing-case. They were not to be seen. There stood the train. Passengers were mounting into it. Old ladies with agitated faces were buying pillows and nibbling biscuits. Elderly gentlemen with yellow countenances and red ribands in their coats were purchasing the*Figaro* and the *Gil Blas*. Children with bare legs were being hauled into compartments. Rook's agent was explaining to a muddled tourist in a tam-o'-shanter the exact difference between the words "Oui" and "Non" The bustle of departure was in the air, but Darrell was not to be seen. Mr. Greyne had left him upon the platform with minute directions as to the point from which the train would start and the hour of its going. Yet he had vanished. The most frantic search, the most frenzied inquiries of officials and total strangers, failed to elicit his whereabouts, and, finally, Mr. Greyne was flung forcibly upward into the *wagonlit*, and caught by the *contrôleur* when the train was actually moving out of the station.

A moment later he fell exhausted upon the pink-plush seat of his compartment, realising his terrible position. He was now utterly alone; without servant, hair-brushes, toothbrushes, razors, sponges, pajamas, shoes. It was a solitude that might be felt. He thought of the sea journey with no kindly hand to minister to him, the arrival in Africa with no humble companion at his side, to wonder with him at the black inhabitants and help him through the customs—to say nothing of the manners. He thought of the dread homes of iniquity into which he must penetrate by night in search of the material for the voracious "Catherine." He had meant to take Darrell with him to them all—Darrell, whose joyful delight in the prospect of exploring the Eastern fastnesses of crime had been so boyish, so truly English in its frank, its even boisterous sincerity.

And now he was utterly alone, almost like Robinson Crusoe.

The *contrôleur* came in to make the bed. Mr. Greyne told him the dreadful story.

"No doubt he has been lured away, monsieur. The dressing-case was of value?"

"Crocodile, gold fittings."

"Probably monsieur will never see him again. As likely as not he will sleep in the Seine to-night, and at the morgue to-morrow."

Mr. Greyne shuddered. This was an ill omen for his expedition. He drank a stiff whisky-and-soda instead of the usual barley water, and went to bed to dream of bloody murders in which he was the victim.

When the train ran into Marseilles next morning he was an unshaven, miserable man.

"Have I time to buy a tooth-brush," he inquired anxiously at the station, "before the boat sails for Algiers?"

The *chef de gare* thought so. Monsieur had four hours, if that was sufficient. Mr. Greyne hastened forth, had a Turkish bath, purchased a new dressing-case, ate a hasty *déjeuner*, and took a cab to the wharf. It was a long drive over the stony streets. He glanced from side to side, watching the bustling traffic, the hurry of the nations going to and from the ships. His eyes rested upon two Arabs who were striding along in his direction. Doubtless they were also bound for Algiers. He thought they looked most wicked, and hastily took a note of them for "African Frailty." Beside his sense of loss and loneliness marched the sense of duty. The great woman at home in Belgrave Square, founder of his fortunes, mother of his children, she depended upon him. Even in his own hour of need he would not fail her. He took a lead pencil, and wrote down:

Saw two Arab ruffians. Bare legs. Look capable of anything. Should not be surprised to hear that they had——

There he paused. That they had what? Done things. Of course, but what things? That was the question. He exerted his imagination, but failed to arrive at any conclusion as to their probable crimes. His knowledge of wickedness was really absurdly limited. For the first time he felt slightly ashamed of it, and began to wish he had gone into the militia. He comforted himself with the thought that in a fortnight he would probably be fit for the regular army. This thought cheered him slightly, and it was with a slight smile upon his face that he welcomed the first glimpse of the *Général Bertrand*, which was lying against the quay ready to cast off at the stroke of noon. Most of the passengers were aboard, but, as Mr. Greyne stepped out of his cab, and prepared to pay the Maltese driver, a trim little lady, plainly dressed in black, and carrying a tiny and rather coquettish hand-bag, was tripping lightly across the gangway. Mr. Greyne glanced at her as he turned to follow, glanced, and then started. That back was surely familiar to him. Where could he have seen it before? He searched his memory as the little lady vanished. It was a smart, even a *chic* back, a back that knew how to take care of itself, a back that need not go through the world alone, a back, in fine, that was most distinctly attractive, if not absolutely alluring. Where had he seen it before, or had he ever seen it at all? He thought of his wife's back, flat, powerful, uncompromising. This was very different, more—how should he put it to himself?—more Algerian, perhaps. He could vaguely conceive it a back such as one might meet with while engaged in adding to one's stock of knowledge of—well—African frailty.

At this moment the steward appeared to show him to his cabin, and his further reflections were mainly connected with the Gulf of Lyons.

Twilight was beginning to fall when, so far as he was capable of thinking, he thought he would like a breath of air. For some moments he lay quite still, dwelling on this idea which had so mysteriously come to him. Then he got up, and thought again, seated upon the cabin floor. He knew there was a deck. He remembered having seen one when he came aboard. He put on his fur coat, still sitting on the cabin floor. The process took some time—he fancied about a couple of years. At last, however, it was completed, and he rose to his feet with the assistance of the washstand and the berth.

The ship seemed very busy, full of almost American activity. He thought a greater calm would have been more decent, and waited in the hope that the floor would presently cease to forget itself. As it showed no symptoms of complying with his desire he endeavoured to spurn it, and, in the fulness of time, gained the companion.

It was very strange, as he remembered afterwards, that only when he had gained the companion did the sense of his utter loneliness rush upon him with overwhelming force: one of the ironies of life, he supposed. Eventually he shook the companion off with a good deal of difficulty, and found himself installed upon planks under a grey sky, and holding fast to a railing, which was all that interposed between him and eternity.

At first he was only conscious of greyness and the noise of winds and waters, but presently a black daub seemed to hover for a second somewhere on the verge of his world, to hover and disappear. He wondered what it was. A smut, perhaps. He rubbed his face. The daub returned. It was very large for a smut. He strove to locate it, and found that it must be somewhere on his left cheek. With a great effort he took out his pocket-handkerchief. Suddenly the daub assumed monstrous proportions. He turned his head, and perceived the lady in black whom he had seen tripping over the gangway on his arrival.

She was a few steps from him, leaning upon the rail in an attitude of the deepest dejection, with her face averted; yet it struck him that her right shoulder was oddly familiar, as her back had surely been. The turn of her head, too—he coughed despairingly. The lady took no notice. He coughed again. Interest was quickening in him. He was determined to see the lady's face.

This time she looked around, showing a pale countenance bedewed with tears, and totally devoid of any expression which he could connect with a consciousness of his presence. For a moment she stared vacantly at him, while he, with almost equal vacancy, regarded her. Then a thrill of surprise shook him. A sudden light of knowledge leaped up in him, and he exclaimed:

"Mademoiselle Verbena!" "Monsieur?" murmured the lady, with an accent of surprise.

"Mademoiselle Verbena! Surely it is—it must be!"

He had staggered sideways, nearing her.

"Mademoiselle Verbena, do you not know me? It is I, Eustace Greyne, the father of your pupils, the husband of Mrs. Eustace Greyne?"

An expression of stark amazement came into the lady's face at these words. She leaned forward till her eyes were close to Mr. Greyne's then gave a little cry.

"*Mon Dieu!* It is true! You are so altered that I could not recognise. And then—what are you doing here, on the wide sea, far from madame?"

"I was just about to ask you the very same question!" cried Mr. Greyne.

IV

"Alas, monsieur!" said Mademoiselle Verbena in her silvery voice, "I go to see my poor mother."

"But I understood that she was dying in Paris."

"Even so. But, when I reached the Rue St. Honoré, I found that they had removed to Algiers. It was the only chance, the doctor said—a warm climate, the sun of Africa. There was no time to let me know. They took her away at once. And now I follow—perhaps to find her dead."

Large tears rolled down her cheeks. Mr. Greyne was deeply affected.

"Let us hope for the best," he exclaimed, seized by a happy inspiration.

The Levantine strove to smile.

"But you, monsieur, why are you here? Ah! perhaps madame is with you! Let me go to her! Let me kiss her dear hands once more——"

Mr. Greyne mournfully checked her fond excitement.

"I am quite alone," he said.

A tragic expression came into the Levantine's face.

"But, then——" she began.

It was impossible for him to tell her about "Catherine." He was, therefore, constrained to subterfuge.

"I—I was suddenly overtaken by—by influenza," he said, in some confusion. "The doctor recommended change of air, of scene."

"He suggested Algiers——"

"*Mon Dieu!* It is like poor mamma!"

"Precisely. Our constitutions are—are doubtless similar. I shall take this opportunity also of improving my knowledge of African manners and—and customs."

A strange smile seemed to dawn for a second on Mademoiselle Verbena's face, but it died instantaneously in a grimace of pain.

"My teeth make me bad," she said. "Ah, monsieur, I must go below, to pray for poor mamma—" she paused, then softly added, "and for monsieur."

She made a movement as if to depart, but Mr. Greyne begged her to remain. In his loneliness the sight even of a Levantine whom he knew solaced his yearning heart. He felt quite friendly towards this poor, unhappy girl, for whom, perhaps, such a shock was preparing upon the distant shore.

"Better stay!" he said. "The air will do you good."

"Ah, if I die, what matter? Unless mamma lives there is no one in the world who cares for me, for whom I care."

"There—there is Mrs. Greyne," said her husband. "And then St. Paul's—remember St. Paul's."

"Ah *ce charmant* St. Paul's! Shall I ever see him more?"

She looked at Mr. Greyne, and suddenly—he knew not why—Mr. Greyne remembered the incident of the diary, and blushed.

"Monsieur has fever!"

Mr. Greyne shook his head. The Levantine eyed him curiously.

"Monsieur wishes to say something to me, and does not like to speak."

Mr. Greyne made an effort. Now that he was with this gentle lady, with her white face, her weeping eyes, her plain black dress, the mere suspicion that she could have opened a locked drawer with a secret key, and filched therefrom a private record, seemed to him unpardonable. Yet, for a brief instant, it had occurred to him, and Mrs. Greyne had seriously held it. He looked at Mademoiselle Verbena, and a sudden impulse to tell her the truth overcame him.

"Yes," he said.

"Tell me, monsieur."

In broken words—the ship was still very busy—Mr. Greyne related the incident of the loss and finding of the diary. As he spoke a slight change stole over the Levantine's face. It certainly became less pale.

"But you have fever now!" cried Mr. Greyne anxiously.

"I! No; I flush with horror, not with fever! The diary, the sacred diary of madame, exposed to view, read by the children, perhaps the servants! That footman, Thomas, with the nose of curiosity! Ah! I behold that nose penetrating into the holy secrets of the existence of madame! I behold it—ah!"

She burst into a fit of hysterics, the laughing species, which is so much more terrible than the other sort. Mr. Greyne was greatly concerned. He lurched to her, and implored her to be calm; but she only laughed the more, while tears streamed down her cheeks. The vision of Thomas gloating over Mrs. Greyne's diary seemed utterly to unnerve her, and Mr. Greyne was able to measure, by this ebullition of horror, the depth of the respect and affection entertained by her for his beloved wife. When, at length, she grew calmer he escorted her towards her cabin, offering her his arm, on which she leaned heavily. As soon as they were in the narrow and heaving passage she turned to him, and said:

"Who can have taken the diary?"

Mr. Greyne blushed again.

"We think it was Thomas," he said.

Mademoiselle Verbena looked at him steadily for a moment, then she cried:

"God bless you, monsieur!"

Mr. Greyne was startled by the abruptness of this pious ejaculation.

"Why?" he inquired.

"You are a good man. You, at least, would not condescend to insult a friendless woman by unworthy suspicions. And madame?"

"Mrs. Greyne"—stammered Mr. Greyne—"is convinced that it was Thomas. In fact—in fact, she was the first to say so."

Mademoiselle Verbena tenderly pressed his hand.

"Madame is an angel. God bless you both!"

She tottered into her cabin, and, as she shut the door, Mr. Greyne heard the terrible, laughing hysterics beginning again.

The next day an influence from Africa seemed spread upon the sea. Calm were the waters, calm and blue. No cloud appeared in the sky. The fierce activities of the ship had ceased, and Mademoiselle Verbena tripped upon the deck at an early hour, to find Mr. Greyne already installed there, and looking positively cheerful. He started up as he perceived her, and chivalrously escorted her to a chair.

Everyone who has made a voyage knows that the sea breeds intimacies. By the time the white houses of Algiers rose on their hill out of the bosom of the waves Mademoiselle Verbena and Mr. Greyne were—shall we say like sister and brother? She had told him all about her childhood in dear Paris, the death of her father the count, murmuring the name of Louis XVI., the poverty of her mother the countess, her own resolve to put aside all aristocratic prejudices and earn her own living. He, in return, had related his Eton days, his momentary bias towards the militia, his marriage—as an innocent youth—with Miss Eugenia Hannibal-Barker. Coming to later times, he was led to confide to the tenderhearted Levantine the fact that he hoped to increase his stock of knowledge while in Africa. Without alluding to "Catherine," he hinted that the cure of influenza was not his only reason for foreign travel.

"I wish to learn something of men and—and women," he murmured in the shell-like ear presented to him. "Of their passions, their desires, their—their follies."

"Ah!" cried Mademoiselle Verbena. "Would that I could assist monsieur! But I am only an ignorant little creature, and know nothing of the world! And I shall be ever at the bedside of mamma."

"You will give me your address? You will let me inquire for the countess?"

"Willingly; but I do not know where I shall be. There will be a message at the wharf. To what hotel goes monsieur?"

"The Grand Hotel."

"I will write there when I have seen mamma. And meanwhile——"

They were coming into harbour. The heights of Mustapha were visible, the woods of the Bois de Boulogne, the towers of the Hotel Splendid.

"Meanwhile, may I beg monsieur not to——" She hesitated.

"Not to what?" asked Mr. Greyne most softly.

"Not to let anyone in England know that I am here?"

She paused. Mr. Greyne was silent, wondering. Mademoiselle Verbena drooped her head.

"The world is so censorious. It might seem strange that I—that monsieur—a man young, handsome, fascinating—the same ship—I have no chaperon—enfin——"

She could get out no more. Her delicacy, her forethought touched Mr. Greyne to tears.

"Not a word," he said. "You are right. The world is evil, and, as you say, I am a—not a word!"

He ventured to press her hand, as an elder brother might have pressed it. For the first time he realised that even to the husband of Mrs. Eustace Greyne the world might attribute—Goodness gracious! What might not the militia think, for instance?

He felt himself, for one moment, potentially a dog.

They parted in a whirl of Arabs on the quay. Mr. Greyne would have stayed to assist Mademoiselle Verbena, but she bade him go.

She whispered that she thought it "better" that they should not seem to—*enfin!*

"I will write to-morrow," she murmured. "*Au revoir!*"

On the last word she was gone. Mr. Greyne saw nothing but Arabs and hotel porters. Loneliness seemed to close in on him once more.

That very evening, after a cup of tea, he presented himself at the office of Rook near the Place du Gouvernement. As he came in he felt a little nervous. There were no tourists in the office, and a courteous clerk with a bright and searching eye at once took him in hand.

"What can we do for you, sir?"

"I am a stranger here," began Mr. Greyne.

"Quite so, sir, quite so."

The clerk twiddled his business-like thumbs, and looked inquiring.

"And being so," Mr. Greyne went on, "it is naturally my wish to see as much of the town as possible; as much as possible, you understand."

"You want a guide? Alphonso!"

Turning, he shouted to an inner room, from which in a moment emerged a short, stout, swarthy personage with a Jewish nose, a French head, an Arab eye with a squint in it, and a markedly Maltese expression.

"This is an excellent guide, sir," said the clerk. "He speaks twenty-five languages."

The stout man, who—as Mr Greyne now perceived—had on a Swiss suit of clothes, a panama hat, and a pair of German elastic-sided boots, confessed in pigeon English, interspersed occasionally with a word or two of something which Mr. Greyne took to be Chinese, that such was undoubtedly the case.

"What do you wish to see? The mosque, the bazaars, St. Eugène, La Trappe, Mustapha, the baths of the Etat-Major, the Jardin d'Essai, the Villa-Anti-Juif, the——"

"One moment!" said Mr. Greyne.

He turned to the clerk.

"May I take a chair?"

"Be seated, sir, pray be seated, and confer with Alphonso."

So saying, he gave himself to an enormous ledger, while Mr. Greyne took a chair opposite to Alphonso, who stood in a Moorish attitude looking apparently in the direction of Marseilles.

"I have come here," said Mr. Greyne, lowering his voice, "with a purpose.".

"You wish to see the Belle Fatma. I will arrange it. She receives every evening in her house in the Rue ——"

"One minute! One minute! You said the something 'Fatma'?"

"The Belle Fatma, the most beautiful woman of Africa. She receives every——"

"Pardon me! One moment! Is this lady——"

Mr. Greyne paused.

"Sir?" said Alphonso, settling his Spanish neck-tie, and gazing steadily towards Marseilles.

"Is this lady—well, sinful?"

Alphonso threw up his hands with a wild Asiatic gesture.

"Sinful! La Belle Fatma! She is a lady of the utmost respectability known to all the town. You go to her house at eight, you take coffee upon the red sofas, you talk with La Belle, you see the dances and hear the music. Do not fear, sir; it is good, it is respectable as England, your country——"

"If it is respectable I don't want to see it," interposed Mr. Greyne. "It would be a waste of time."

The clerk lifted his head from the ledger, and Alphonso, by means of standing with his back almost square to Mr. Greyne, and looking over his right shoulder, succeeded at length in fixing his eye upon him.

"I have not travelled here to see respectable things," continued Mr. Greyne, with a slight blush. "Quite the contrary."

"Sir?"

The voice of Alphonso seemed to have changed, to have taken on a hard, almost a menacing tone. Mr. Greyne thought of his beloved wife, of Merrin's exercise-books, and clenched his hands, endeavouring to feel, and to go on, like a militiaman.

"Quite the contrary," he repeated firmly; "my object in coming to Africa is to—to search about in the Kasbah, and the disrep——"

He choked, recovered himself, and continued: "Disreputable quarters of Algiers—hem——"

"What for, sir?"

The voice of Alphonso was certainly changed.

"What for?" said Mr. Greyne, growing purple. "For frailty."

"Sir?"

"For frailty—for wickedness."

A slight cackle emanated from the ledger, but immediately died away. A dead silence reigned in the office, broken only by the distant sound of the sea, and by the hard breathing of Alphonso, who had suddenly begun to pant.

"I wish to go to all the wicked places—*all!*"

The ledger cackled again more audibly. Mr. Greyne felt a prickling sensation run over him, but the thought of "Catherine" nerved him to his awful task.

"It is my wife's express desire that I should do so," he added desperately, quite forgetting Mrs. Greyne's injunction to keep her dark in his desire to stand well with Rook's.

The ledger went off into a hyena imitation, and Alphonso, turning still more away from Mr. Greyne, so as to get the eye fuller upon him, exclaimed, in a mixture of Aryan and Eurasian languages:

"Sir, I am a respectable, unmarried man. I was born in Buenos Ayres, educated in Smyrna, came of age in Constantinople, and have practised as guide in Bagdad and other particular cities. I refuse to have anything to do with you and your wife."

So saying, he bounced into the inner room, and banged the door, while the ledger gave itself up to peals of merriment, and Mr. Greyne tottered forth upon the sea-front, bathed in a cold perspiration, and feeling more guilty than a murderer.

It was a staggering blow. He leaned over the stone parapet of the low wall, and let the soft breezes from the bay flit through his hair, and thought of Mrs. Greyne spurned by Alphonso. What was he to do? Kicked out of Rook's, to whom could he apply? There must be wickedness in Algiers, but where? He saw none, though night was falling and stout Frenchmen were already intent upon their absinthe.

"Does monsieur wish to see the Kasbah to-night?"

Was it a voice from heaven? He turned, and saw standing beside him a tall, thin, audacious-looking young man, with coal-black moustaches, magnificent eyes, and an air that was half-languid, half-serpentine.

"Who are you?"

"I am a guide, monsieur. Here are my certificates."

He produced from the inner pocket of his coat a large bundle of dirty papers.

"If monsieur will deign to look them over."

But Mr. Greyne waved them away. What did he care for Certificates? Here was a guide to African frailty. That was sufficient. He was in a desperate mood, and uttered desperate words.

"Look here," he said rapidly, "are you wicked?"

"Very wicked, monsieur."

"Good!"

"Wicked, monsieur."

"Right!"

"Wrong, monsieur."

"I mean that it is good for me that you are wicked."

"Monsieur is very good."

"Yes; but I wish to be—that is, to see the other thing. Can you undertake to show me everything shocking in Algiers?"

"But certainly, monsieur. For a consideration."

"Name your price."

"Two hundred pounds, monsieur."

Mr. Greyne started. It seemed a high figure.

"Monsieur thought it would be more? I make a special price, because I have taken a fancy to monsieur. I remove fifty pounds. Monsieur, of course, will pay all expenses."

"Of course, of course."

It was no time to draw back.

"How long will it take?"

"To see all the shocking—?"

"Precisely."

"There is a good deal. A fortnight, three weeks. It depends on monsieur. If he is strong, and can do without sleep——"

"We shall have to be up at night?"

"Naturally."

"I shall go to bed during the day, and get through it in a fortnight."

"Perfectly."

"Be at the Grand Hotel to-night at ten o'clock precisely."

"At ten o'clock I will be there. Monsieur will pay a little in advance?"

"Here are twenty pounds," cried Mr. Greyne recklessly.

The audacious-looking young man took the notes with decision, made a graceful salute, and disappeared in the direction of the quay, while Mr. Greyne walked to his hotel, flushed with excitement, and feeling like the most desperate criminal in Africa. If the militia could see him now!

At dinner he drank a bottle of champagne, and afterwards smoked a strong cigar over his coffee and liqueur. As he was finishing these frantic enjoyments the head waiter—a personage bearing a strong resemblance to an enlarged edition of Napoleon the First—approached him rather furtively, and, bending down, whispered in his ear:

"A gentleman has called to take monsieur to the Kasbah."

Mr. Greyne started, and flushed a guilty red.

"I will come in a moment," he answered, trying to assume a nonchalant voice, such as that in which a hardened major of dragoons announces that in his time he was a devil of a fellow.

The head waiter retired, looking painfully intelligent, and Mr. Greyne sprang upstairs, seized a Merrin's exercise-book and a lead pencil, put on a dark overcoat, popped one of the Springfield revolvers into the pocket of it, and hastened down into the hall of the hotel, where the audacious-looking young man was standing, surrounded by saucy chasseurs in gay liveries and peaked caps, by Algerian waiters, and by German-Swiss porters, all of whom were smiling and looking choke-full of sympathetic comprehension.

"Ha!" said Mr. Greyne, still in the major's, voice. "There you are!"

"Behold me, monsieur."

"That's good."

"Wicked, monsieur."

"Well, let's be off to the mosque."

One of the chasseurs—a child of eight who was thankful that he knew no better—burst into a piping laugh. The waiters turned hastily away, and the German-Swiss porters retreated to the bureau with some activity.

"To the mosque—precisely, monsieur," returned the guide, with complete self-possession.

They stepped out at once upon the pavement, where a carriage was in waiting.

"Where are we going?" inquired Mr. Greyne in an anxious voice.

"We are going to the heights to see the Ouled," replied the guide. "*En avant!*"

He bounded in beside Mr. Greyne, the coachman cracked his whip, the horses trotted. They were off upon their terrible pilgrimage.

V

On the following afternoon, at a quarter to three, when Mr. Greyne came down to breakfast, he found, lying beside the boiled eggs, a note directed to him in a feminine handwriting. He tote it open with trembling fingers, and read as follows:—

1 Rue du Petit Neore.

Dear Monsieur,—I am here. Poor mamma is in the hospital. I

am allowed to see her twice a day. At all other times I

remain alone, praying and weeping. I trust that monsieur has

passed a good night. For me, I was sleepless, thinking of

mamma. I go now to church.

Adele Verbena.

He laid this missive down, and sighed deeply. How strangely innocent it was, how simple, how sincere! There were white souls in Algiers—yes, even in Algiers. Strange that he should know one! Strange that he, who had filled a Merrin's exercise-book with tiny writing, and had even overflowed on to the cover after "crossing" many pages, should receive the child-like confidences of one! "I go now to the church." Tears came into his eyes as he laid the letter down beside a pile of buttered toast over which the burning afternoon sun of Africa was shining.

"Monsieur will take milk and sugar?"

It was the head waiter's Napoleonic voice. Mr. Greyne controlled himself. The man was smiling intelligently. All the staff of the hotel smiled intelligently at Mr. Greyne to-day—the waiters, the porters, the chasseurs. The child of eight who was thankful that he knew no better had greeted him with a merry laugh as he came down to breakfast, and an "*Oh, là, là!*" which had elicited a rebuke from the proprietor. Indeed, a wave of human sympathy flowed upon Mr. Greyne, whose ashy face and dull, washed-out eyes betrayed the severity of his night-watch.

"Monsieur will feel better after a little food."

The head waiter handed the buttered toast with bland majesty, at the same time shooting a reproving glance at the little chasseur, who was peeping from behind the door at the afternoon breakfaster.

"I feel perfectly well," replied Mr. Greyne, with an attempt at cheerfulness.

"Still, monsieur will feel much better after a little food."

Mr. Greyne began to toy with an egg.

"You know Algiers?" he asked.

"I was born here, monsieur. If monsieur wishes to explore to-night again the Kasbah I can——"

But Mr. Greyne stopped him with a gesture that was almost fierce.

"Where is the Rue du Petit Nègre?"

"Monsieur wishes to go there to-night?"

"I wish to go there now, directly I have finished break—lunch."

The head waiter's face was wreathed with humorous surprise.

"But monsieur is wonderful—superb! Never have I seen a traveller like monsieur!"

He gazed at Mr. Greyne with tropical appreciation.

"Monsieur had better have a carriage. The street is difficult to find."

"Order me one. I shall start at once."

Mr. Greyne pushed away the sunlit buttered toast, and got up.

"Monsieur is superb. Never have I seen a traveller like monsieur!" Napoleon's voice was almost reverent. He hastened out, followed slowly by Mr. Greyne.

"A carriage for monsieur! Monsieur desires to go to the Rue du Petit Nègre!"

The staff of the hotel gathered about the door as if to speed a royal personage, and Mr. Greyne noticed that their faces too were touched with an almost startled reverence. He stepped into the carriage, signed feebly, but with determination, to the Arab coachman, and was driven away, followed by a parting "*Oh, là là!*" from the chasseur, uttered in a voice that sounded shrill with sheer amazement.

Through winding, crowded streets he went, by bazaars and Moorish bath-houses, mosques and Catholic churches, barracks and cafés, till at length the carriage turned into an alley that crept up a steep hill. It moved on a little way, and then stopped.

"Monsieur must descend here," said the coachman. "Mount the steps, go to the right and then to the left. Near the summit of the hill he will find the Rue du Petit Nègre. Shall I wait for monsieur?"

"Yes."

The coachman began to make a cigarette, while Mr. Greyne set forth to follow his directions, and, at length, stood before an arch, which opened into a courtyard adorned with orange-trees in tubs, and paved with blue and white tiles. Around this courtyard was a three-storey house with a flat roof, and from a bureau near a little fountain a stout Frenchwoman called to demand his business. He asked for Mademoiselle Verbena, and was at once shown into a saloon lined with chairs covered with yellow rep, and begged to take a seat. In two minutes Mademoiselle Verbena appeared, drying her eyes with a tiny pocket-handkerchief, and forcing a little pathetic smile of welcome. Mr. Greyne clasped her hand in silence. She sat down in a rep chair at his right, and they looked at each other.

"*Mais, mon Dieu!* How monsieur is changed!" cried the Levantine. "If madame could see him! What has happened to monsieur?"

"Miss Verbena," replied Mr. Greyne, "I have seen the Ouled on the heights."

A spasm crossed the Levantine's face. She put her handkerchief to it for a moment. "What is an Ouled?" she inquired, withdrawing it.

"I dare not tell you," he replied solemnly.

"But indeed I wish to know, so that I may sympathise with monsieur."

Mr. Greyne hesitated, but his heart was full; he felt the need of sympathy. He looked at Mademoiselle Verbena, and a great longing to unburden himself overcame him.

"An Ouled," he replied, "is a dancing-girl from the desert of Sahara."

"*Mon Dieu!* How does she dance? Is it a valse, a polka, a quadrille?" "No. Would that it were!" And Mr. Greyne, unable further to govern his desire for full expression, gave Mademoiselle Verbena a slightly Bowdlerised description of the dances of the desert. She heard him with amazement.

"How terrible!" she exclaimed when he had finished. "And does one pay much to see such steps of the Evil One?"

"I gave her twenty pounds. Abdallah Jack——"

"Abdallah Jack?"

"My guide informed me that was the price. He tells me it is against the law, and that each time an Ouled dances she risks being thrown into prison."

"Poor lady! How sad to have to earn one's bread by such devices, instead of by teaching to the sweet little ones of monsieur the sympathetic grammar of one's native country."

Mr. Greyne was touched to the quick by this allusion, which brought, as in a vision, the happy home in Belgrave Square before him.

"You are an angel!" he exclaimed.

Mademoiselle Verbena shook her head.

"And this poor Ouled, you will go to her again?

"Yes. It seems that she is in communication with all the—the—well, all the odd people of Algiers, and that one can only get at them through her."

"Indeed?"

"Abdallah Jack tells me that while I am here I should pay her a weekly salary, and that, in return, I shall see all the terrible ceremonies of the Arabs. I have decided to do so——

"Ah, you have decided!"

For a moment Mr. Greyne started. There seemed a new sound in Mademoiselle Verbena's voice, a gleam in her dark brown eyes.

"Yes," he said, looking at her in wonder. "But I have not yet told Abdallah Jack."

The Levantine looked gently sad again.

"Ah," she said in her usual pathetic voice, "how my heart bleeds for this poor Ouled. By the way, what is her name?"

"Aishoush."

"She is beautiful?"

"I hardly know. She was so painted, so tattooed, so very—so very different from Mrs. Eustace Greyne."

"How sad! How terrible! Ah, but you must long for the dear bonnet strings of madame?"

Did he? As she spoke Mr. Greyne asked himself the question. Shocked as he was, fatigued by his researches, did he wish that he were back again in Belgrave Square, drinking barley water, pasting notices of his wife's achievements into the new album, listening while she read aloud from the manuscript of her latest novel? He wondered, and—how strange, how almost terrible—he was not sure.

"Is it not so?" murmured Mademoiselle Verbena.

"Naturally I miss my beloved wife," said Mr. Greyne with a certain awkwardness. "How is your poor, dear mother?"

Tears came at once into the Levantine's eyes.

"Very, very ill, monsieur. Still there is a chance—just a chance that she may not die. Ah, when I sit here all alone in this strange place, I feel that she will perish, that soon I shall be quite deserted in this cruel, cruel world!"

The tears began to flow down her cheeks with determination. Mr. Greyne was terribly upset.

"You must cheer up," he exclaimed. "You must hope for the best."

"Sitting here alone, how can I?"

She sobbed.

"Sitting here alone—very true!"

A sudden thought, a number of sudden thoughts, struck him.

"You must not sit here alone."

"Monsieur!"

"You must come out. You must drive. You must see the town, distract yourself."

"But how? Can a—a girl go about alone in Algiers?"

"Heaven forbid! No; I will escort you."

"Monsieur!"

A smile of innocent, girlish joy transformed her face, but suddenly she was grave again.

"Would it be right, *convenable?*"

Mr. Greyne was reckless. The dog potential rose up in him again.

"Why not? And, besides, who knows us here? Not a soul."

"That is true."

"Put on your bonnet. Let us start at once!"

"But I do not wear the bonnet. I am not like madame."

"To be sure. Your hat."

And as she flew to obey him, Mr. Eustace Greyne found himself impiously thanking the powers that be for this strange chance of going on the spree with a toque. When Mademoiselle Verbena returned he was looking almost rakish. He eyed her neat black hat and close-fitting black jacket with a glance not wholly unlike that of a militiaman. In her hand she held a vivid scarlet parasol.

"Monsieur," she said, "it is terrible, this *ombrelle*, when mamma lies at death's door. But what can I do? I have no other, and cannot afford to buy one. The sun is fierce. I dare not expose myself to it without a shelter."

She seemed really distressed as she opened the parasol, and spread the vivid silk above her pretty black-clothed figure; but Mr. Greyne thought the effect was brilliant, and ventured to say so. As they passed the bureau by the fountain on their way out the stout Frenchwoman cast an approving glance at Mademoiselle Verbena.

"The little rat will not see much more of the little negro now," she murmured to herself. "After all the English have their uses."

VI

In Belgrave Square Mrs. Eustace Greyne was beginning to get slightly uneasy. Several things combined to make her so. In the first place, Mademoiselle Verbena had never returned from her mother's Parisian bedside, and had not even written a line to say how the dear parent was, and when the daughter's nursing occupation was likely to be over. In the second place, Adolphus, in consequence of the Levantine's absence, had totally lost his grasp, always uncertain, upon the irregular verbs. In the third place, Darrell, the valet, had returned to London the day after his departure from it, minus not only his master's dressing-case, but minus everything he possessed. His story was that, while waiting at the station in Paris for his master's appearance, he had entered into conversation with an agreeable stranger, and been beguiled into the acceptance of an absinthe at a café just outside. After swallowing the absinthe he remembered nothing more till he came to himself in a deserted waiting-room at the Gare du Nord, back to which he had been mysteriously conveyed. In his pocket was no money, no watch, only the return half of a second-class ticket from London to Paris. He, therefore, wandered about the streets till morning broke, and then came back to London a crestfallen and miserable man, bemoaning his untoward fate, and cursing "them blasted Frenchies" from the bottom of his British heart.

Mrs. Greyne's anxiety on her husband's behalf, now that he was thrown absolutely unattended upon the inhospitable shores of Africa, was not lessened by a fourth circumstance, which, indeed, worried her far more than all the others put together. This was Mr. Greyne's prolonged absence from her side. Precisely one calendar month had now elapsed since he had buried his face in her prune bonnet strings at Victoria Station, and there seemed no prospect of his return. He wrote to her, indeed, frequently, and his letters were full of wistful regret and longing to be once more safe in the old homestead in Belgrave Square, drinking barley water, and pasting Romeike & Curtice notices into the new album which lay, gaping for him, upon the table of his sanctum. But he did not come; nay, more, he wrote plainly that there was no prospect of his coming for the present. It seemed that the wickedness of Africa was very difficult to come at. It did not lie upon the surface, but was hidden far down in depths to which the ordinary tourist found it almost impossible to penetrate. In his numerous letters Mr. Greyne described his heroic and unremitting exertions to fill the Merrin's note-books with matter that would be suitable for the purging of humanity. He set out in full his interview with Alphonso at the office of Rook, and his definite rejection by that cosmopolitan official. According to the letters, after this event he had spent no less than a fortnight searching in vain for any sign of wickedness in the Algerian capital. He had frequented the cafés, the public bars, the theatres, the churches. He had been to the Velodrome. He had sat by the hour in the Jardin d'Essai. At night he had strolled in the fairs and hung about the circus. Yet nowhere had he been able to perceive anything but the most innocent pleasure, the simple merriment of a gay and guileless population to whom the idea of crime seemed as foreign as the idea of singing the English national anthem.

During the third week it was true that matters—always according to Mr. Greyne's letters home—slightly improved. While walking near the quay, in active search for nautical outrage, he saw an Arab dock labourer, who had been over-smoking kief, run amuck, and knock down a couple of respectable snake-charmers who were on the point of embarkation for Tunis with their reptiles. This incident had filed up a half-score of pages in exercise-book number one, and had flooded Mr. Greyne with hope and aspiration. But it was followed by a stagnant lull which had lasted for days and had only been disturbed by the trifling incident of a gentleman in the Jewish quarter of the town setting fire to a neighbour's bazaar, in the very natural endeavour to find a French half-penny which he had chanced to drop among a bale of carpets while looking in to drive a soft bargain. As Mrs. Greyne wired to Algiers, such incidents were of no value to "Catherine."

A very active interchange of views had gone on between the husband and wife as time went by, and the book was at a standstill. At first Mrs. Greyne contented herself with daily letters, but latterly she had resorted to wires, explanatory, condemnatory, hortatory, and even comminatory. She began bitterly to regret her husband's well-proven innocence, and wished she had despatched an uncle of hers by marriage, an ex-captain in the Royal Navy, who, she began to feel certain, would have been able to find far more frailty in Algiers than poor Eustace, in his simplicity, would ever come at. She even began to wish that she had crossed the sea in person, and herself boldly set about the ingathering of the material for which she was so impatiently waiting.

Her uneasiness was brought to a head by a letter from a house agent, stating that the corner mansion in Park Lane next to the Duke of Ebury's was being nibbled at by a Venezuelan millionaire. She wired this terrible fact at once to Africa, adding, at an enormous expenditure of cash:

This will never do. You are too innocent, and cannot see

what lies before you. Obtain assistance. Go to the British

consul.

Mr. Greyne at once cabled back:

Am following your advice. Will wire result. Regret my

innocence, but am distressed that you should so utterly

condemn it.

Upon receiving this telegram at night, before a lonely dinner, Mrs. Eustace Greyne was deeply moved. She felt she had been hasty. She knew that to very few women was it given to have a husband so free from all masculine infirmities as Mr. Greyne. At the same time there was "Catherine," there was the mansion in Park Lane, there was the Venezuelan millionaire. She began to feel distracted, and, for the first time in her life, refused to partake of sweetbreads fried in mushroom ketchup, a dish which she had greatly affected from the time when she wrote her first short story. While she was in the very act of waving away this delicacy a footman came in with a foreign telegram. She opened it quickly, and read as follows:—

British consul horrified; was ignominiously expelled from

consulate; great scandal; am much upset, but will never give

in, for your sake.   *Eustace.*

As the dread meaning of these words penetrated at length to Mrs. Greyne's voluminous brain a deep flush overspread her noble features. She rose from the table with a determination that struck awe to the hearts of the powdered underlings, and, drawing herself up to her full height, exclaimed:

"Send Mrs. Forbes at once to my study, if you please—at once, do you understand?"

In a moment Mrs. Forbes, who was the great novelist's maid, appeared on the threshold of the oracle's lair. She was a sober-looking, black-silk personage, who always wore a pork-pie cap in the house, and a Mother Hubbard bonnet out of it. Having been in service with Mrs. Greyne ever since the latter penned her last minor poetry—Mrs. Greyne had been a minor poet for three years soon after she put her hair up—Mrs. Forbes had acquired a certain literary expression of countenance and a manner that was decidedly prosy. She read a good deal after her supper of an evening, and was wont to be the arbiter when any literary matter was discussed in the servants' hall.

"Madam?" she said, respectfully entering the room, and bending the pork-pie cap forward in an attentive attitude.

Mrs. Greyne was silent for a moment. She appeared to be thinking deeply. Mrs. Forbes gently closed the door, and sighed. It was nearly her supper-time, and she felt pensive.

"Madam?" she said again.

Mrs. Greyne looked up. A strange fire burned in her large eyes.

"Mrs. Forbes," she said at length, with weighty deliberation, "the mission of woman in the world is a great one."

"Very true, madam. My own words to Butler Phillips no longer ago than dinner this midday."

"It is the protecting of man—neither more nor less."

"My own statement, madam, to Second Footman Archibald this self-same day at the tea-board."

"Man needs guidance, and looks for it to us—or rather to me."

At the last word Mrs. Forbes pinched her lips together, and appeared older than her years and sourer than her normal temper.

"At this moment, Mrs. Forbes," continued Mrs. Greyne, with rising fervour, "he looks for it to me from Africa. From that dark continent he stretches forth his hands to me in humble supplication."

"Mr. Greyne has not been taken with another of his bilious attacks, I hope, madam?" said Mrs. Forbes.

Mrs. Greyne smiled. The ignorance of the humbly born entertained her. It was so simple, so transparent.

"You fail to understand me," she answered. "But never mind; others have done the same."

She thought of her reviewers. Mrs. Forbes smiled. She also could be entertained.

"Madam?" she inquired once more after a pause.

"I shall leave for Africa to-morrow morning," said Mrs. Greyne. "You will accompany me."

There was a dead silence.

"You will accompany me. Do you understand? Obtain assistance from the housemaids in the packing. Select my quietest gowns, my least conspicuous bonnets. I have my reasons for wishing, while journeying to Africa and remaining there, to pass, if possible, unnoticed."

Again there was a pause. Mrs. Greyne looked up at Mrs. Forbes, and observed a dogged expression upon her countenance.

"What is the matter?" she asked the maid.

"Do we go by Paris, madam?" said Mrs. Forbes.

"Certainly."

"Then, madam, I'm very sorry, but I couldn't risk it, not if it was ever so——"

"Why not? Why this fear of Lutetia?"

"Madam, I'm not afraid of any Lutetia as ever wore apron, but to go to Paris to be drugged with absint, and put away in a third-class waiting-room like a package—I couldn't madam, not even if I have to leave your service."

Mrs. Greyne recognised that the episode of the valet had struck home to the lady's maid.

"But you will not leave my side."

"They will absint you, madam."

"But you will travel first in a sleeping-car."

Mrs. Forbes put up her hand to her pork-pie cap, as if considering.

"Very well, madam, to oblige you I will undergo it," she said at length. "But I would not do the like for another living lady."

"I will raise your wages. You are a faithful creature."

"Does master expect us, madam?" asked Mrs. Forbes as she prepared to retire.

A bright and tender look stole into Mrs. Greyne's intellectual face.

"No," she replied.

She turned her large and beaming eyes full upon the maid.

"Mrs. Forbes," she said, with an amount of emotion that was very rare in her, "I am going to tell you a great truth."

"Madam?" said Mrs. Forbes respectfully.

"The sweetest moments of life, those which lift man nearest heaven, and make him thankful for the great gift of existence, are sometimes those which are unforeseen."

She was thinking of Mr. Greyne's ecstasy when, upon the inhospitable African shore where he was now enduring such tragic misfortunes, he perceived the majestic form of his loved one—his loved one whom he believed to be in Belgrave Square—coming towards him to soothe, to comfort, to direct. She brushed away a tear.

"Go, Mrs. Forbes," she said.

And Mrs. Forbes retired, smiling.

An epic might well be written on the great novelist's journey to Africa, upon her departure from Charing Cross, shrouded in a black gauze veil, her silent thought as the good ship *Empress* rode cork-like upon the Channel waves, her ascetic lunch—a captain's biscuit and a glass of water—at the buffet at Calais, her arrival in Paris when the shades of night had fallen. An epic might well be written. Perhaps some day it will be, by herself.

In Paris she suffered a good deal on account of Mrs. Forbes, who, in her fear of "absint," became hysterical, and caused not a little annoyance by accusing various inoffensive French travellers of nefarious designs upon her property and person. In the Gulf of Lyons she suffered even more, and as, unluckily, the wind was contrary and the sea prodigious during the whole of the passage across the Mediterranean, both she and Mrs. Forbes arrived at Algiers four hours late, in a condition which may be more easily imagined than properly described.

Genius in thrall to the body, and absolutely dependent upon green chartreuse for its flickering existence, is no subject for even a sympathetic pen. Sufficient to say that, when the ship came in under the lights of Algiers, the crowd of shouting Arabs was struck to silence by the spectacle of Mrs. Greyne and Mrs. Forbes endeavouring to disembark, in bonnets that were placed seaward upon the head instead of landward, unbuttoned boots, and gowns soaked with the attentions of the waves.

After being gently and permanently relieved of their light hand-baggage, the mistress and maid, who seemed greatly overwhelmed by the sight of Africa, and who moved—or rather were carried—as in a dream, were placed reverently in the nearest omnibus, and conveyed to the farthest hotel, which was situated upon a lofty hill above the town. Here a slightly painful scene took place.

Having been assisted by the staff into a Moorish hall, Mrs. Greyne inquired in a reticent voice for her husband, and was politely informed that there was no person of the name of Greyne in the hotel. For a moment she seemed threatened with dissolution, but with a supreme effort calling upon her mighty brain she surmised that her husband was possibly passing under a pseudonym in order to throw America off the scent. She, therefore, demanded to have the guests then present in the hotel at once paraded before her. As there was some difficulty about this—the guests being then at dinner—she whispered for the visitors' book, thinking that, perchance, Mr. Greyne had inscribed his name there, and that the staff, being foreign, did not recognise it as murmured by herself. The book was brought, upon its cover in golden letters the words: "Hôtel Loubet et Majestic." Then explanations of a somewhat disagreeable nature occurred, and Mrs. Greyne and Mrs. Forbes, after a heavy payment had been exacted for their conveyance to a place they had desired not to go to, were carried forth, and consigned to another vehicle, which at length brought them, on the stroke of nine, to the Grand Hotel.

Having been placed reverently in the brilliantly-lighted hall, they were surrounded by the proprietor, the *maître d'hôtel* and his assistants, the porters, and the chasseurs, with all of whom Mr. Greyne was now familiar. Brandy and water having been supplied, together with smelling-salts and burnt feathers, Mrs. Greyne roused herself from an acute attack of lethargy, and asked for Mr. Greyne. A joyous smile ran round the circle.

"Monsieur Greyne," said the proprietor, "who is living here for the winter?" 4

"Mr. Eustace Greyne," murmured the great novelist, grasping her bonnet with both hands.

The *maître d'hôtel* drew nearer.

"Madame wishes to see Monsieur Greyne?" he asked.

"I do—at once."

A blessed consciousness of Mother Earth was gradually beginning to steal over her. She even strove feebly to sit up on her chair, a German-Swiss porter of enormous size assisting her.

"But Monsieur Greyne is out."

"Out?"

"Yes, madame. Monsieur Greyne is always out at night."

The eyes of the little chasseur who knew no better began to twinkle. Mrs. Forbes gave a slight cough. Tears filled the novelist's eyes.

"God bless my Eustace!" she murmured, deeply touched by this evidence of his devotion to her interests.

"Madame says——" asked the proprietor.

"Where does Mr. Greyne go?" inquired the novelist.

"To the Kasbah, madame."

"I knew it!" cried Mrs. Greyne, with returning animation. "I knew it would be so!"

"Madame is acquainted with Monsieur Greyne?" said the *maître d'hôtel*, while the little crowd gathered more closely about the wave-worn group.

"I am Mrs. Eustace Greyne," returned the great novelist recklessly. "I am the wife of Mr. Eustace Greyne."

There was a moment of supreme silence. Then a loud, an even piercing "*Oh, là, là,* broke upon the air, succeeded instantaneously by a burst of laughter that seemed to thrill with all the wild blessedness of boyhood. It came, of course, from the little chasseur; it came, and stayed. Nothing could stop it, and eventually the happy child had to be carried forth upon the sea-front to enjoy his innocent mirth at leisure and in solitude beneath the African stars. Mrs. Greyne did not notice his disappearance. She was intent upon important matters.

"At what time does Mr. Greyne usually set forth?" she asked of the proprietor, whose face now bore a strangely twisted appearance, as if afflicted by a toothache.

"Immediately after dinner, madame, if not before. Of late it has generally been before."

"And he stays out late?"

"Very late, madame."

The twisted appearance began to seem infectious. It was visible upon the faces of most of those surrounding Mrs. Greyne and Mrs. Forbes. Indeed, even the latter showed some signs of it, although the large shadow cast over her features by the hind side of her Mother Hubbard bonnet to some extent disguised them from the public view.

"Till what hour?" pursued Mrs. Greyne in a voice of almost yearning tenderness and pity.

"Well, madame"—the proprietor displayed some slight confusion—"I really can hardly say. The *maître d'hôtel* can perhaps inform you."

Mrs. Greyne turned her ox-like eyes upon the enlarged edition of Napoleon the First.

"Monsieur Greyne seldom returns before seven or eight o'clock in the morning, madame. He then retires to bed, and comes down to breakfast at about four o'clock in the afternoon."

Mrs. Greyne was touched to the very quick. Her husband was sacrificing his rest, his health—nay, perhaps even his very life—in her service. It was well she had come, well that a period was to be put to these terrible researches. They should be stopped at once, even this very night. Better a thousand literary failures than that her husband's existence should be placed in jeopardy. She rose suddenly from her chair, tottered, gasped, recovered herself, and spoke.

"Prepare dinner for me at once," she said, "and order a carriage and a competent guide to be before the door in half-an-hour."

"Madame is going out? But madame is ill, tired!"

"It matters not."

"Where does madame wish to go?"

"I am going to the Kasbah to find my husband."

"I will escort madame."

The proprietor, the *maître d'hôtel*, the waiters, the porters, the chasseurs, Mrs. Greyne and Mrs. Forbes, all turned about to face the determined speaker.

And there before them, his dark eyes gleaming, his long moustaches bristling fiercely—here stood Abdallah Jack.

VII

Man is a self-deceiver. It must, therefore, ever be a doubtful point whether Mr. Eustace Greyne, during his residence in Africa, absolutely lost sight of his sense of duty; whether, beguiled by the lively attentions of a fiercely foreign town, he deliberately resolved to take his pleasure regardless of consequences and of the sacred ties of Belgrave Square. We prefer to think that some vague idea of combining two duties—that which he owed to himself and that which he owed to Mrs. Greyne—moved him in all he did, and that the subterfuge into which he was undoubtedly led was not wholly selfish, not wholly criminal. Nevertheless, that he had lied to his beloved wife is certain. Even while she sat over a cutlet and a glass of claret in the white-and-gold dining-room of the Grand Hotel, preparatory to her departure to the Kasbah with Abdallah Jack, the dozen of Merrin's exercise-books lay upstairs in Mr. Greyne's apartments filled to the brim with African frailty. Already there was material enough in their pages to furnish forth a library of "Catherines." Yet Mr. Greyne still lingered far from his home, and wired to that home fabricated accounts of the singular innocence of Algiers. He even allowed it to be supposed that his own innocence stood in the way of his fulfilment of Mrs. Greyne's behests—he who could now have given points in knowledge of the world to whole regiments of militiamen!

It was not right, and, doubtless, he must stand condemned by every moralist. But let it not be forgotten that he had fallen under the influence of a Levantine.

Mademoiselle Verbena's mother, hidden in some unnamed hospital of Algiers, appeared to be one of those ingenious elderly ladies who can hover indefinitely upon the brink of death without actually dying. During the whole time that Mr. Greyne had been in Africa her state had been desperate, yet she still clung to life. As her daughter said, she possessed extraordinary vitality, and this vitality seemed to have been inherited by her child. Despite her grave anxieties Mademoiselle Verbena succeeded in sustaining a remarkable cheeriness, and even a fascinating vivacity, when in the company of others. As she said to Mr. Greyne, she did not think it right to lay her burdens upon the shoulders of her neighbours. She, therefore, forced herself to appear contented, even at various moments gay, when she and Mr. Greyne were lunching, dining, or supping together, were driving upon the front, sailing upon the azure waters of the bay, riding upon the heights beyond El-Biar, or, ensconced in a sumptuous private box, listening to the latest French farce at one or another of the theatres. Only one day, when they had driven out to the monastery at La Trappe de Staouëli, did a momentary cloud descend upon her piquant features, and she explained this by the frank confession that she had always wished to become a nun, but had been hindered from following her vocation by the necessity of earning money to support her aged parents. Mr. Greyne had never seen the Ouled since his first evening in Algiers, but he still paid her a weekly salary, through Abdallah Jack, who explained to him that the interesting lady, in a discreet retirement, was perpetually occupied in arranging the exhibitions of African frailty at which he so frequently assisted. She was, in fact, earning her liberal salary. Mademoiselle Verbena and Abdallah Jack had met on several occasions, and Mr. Greyne had introduced the latter to the former as his guide, and had generously praised his abilities; but in Mademoiselle Verbena took very little notice of him, and, as time went on, Abdallah Jack seemed to conceive a most distressing dislike of her. On several occasions he advised Mr. Greyne not to frequent her company so assiduously, and when Mr. Greyne asked him to explain the meaning of his monitions he took refuge in vague generalities and Eastern imagery. He had a profound contempt for women as companions, which grieved Mr. Greyne's Western ideas, and evidently thought that Mademoiselle Verbena ought to be clapped forthwith into a long veil, and put away in a harem behind an iron grille. When Mr. Greyne explained the English point of view Abdallah Jack took refuge in a sulky silence; but during the week immediately preceding the arrival of Mrs. Greyne his temper had become actively bad, and Mr. Greyne began seriously to consider whether it would not be better to pay him a last *douceur*, and tell him to go about his business.

Before doing this, however, Mr. Greyne desired to have one more interview with the mysterious Ouled on the heights, to whom he owed the knowledge which would henceforth enable him to cut out the militia. He said so to Abdallah Jack. The latter agreed sulkily to arrange it; and matters so fell out that on the night of Mrs. Greyne's arrival her husband was seated in a room in one of the remotest houses of the Kasbah, watching the Ouled's mysterious evolutions, while Mademoiselle Verbena—as she herself had informed Mr.4 Greyne—sat in the hospital by the bedside of her still dying mother. Abdallah Jack had apparently been most anxious to assist at Mr. Greyne's interview with the Ouled, but Mr. Greyne had declined to allow this. The evil temper of the guide was beginning to get thoroughly upon his employer's nerves, and even the natural desire to have an interpreter at hand was overborne by the dislike of Abdallah Jack's morose eyes and sarcastic speeches about women. Moreover, the Ouled spoke a word or two of uncertain French.

Thus, therefore, things fell out, and such was the precise situation when Mrs. Greyne flicked a crumb from her chocolate brocade gown, tied her bonnet strings, and rose from table to set forth to the Kasbah with Abdallah Jack.

It was a radiant night. In the clear sky the stars shone brilliantly, looking down upon the persistent convulsions of the little chasseur, who had not yet recovered from his attack of merriment on learning who Mrs. Greyne was. The sea, quite calm now that the great novelist was no longer upon it, lapped softly along the curving shores of the bay. The palm-trees of the town garden where the band plays on warm evenings waved lazily in the soft and scented breeze. The hooded figures of the Arabs lounged against the stone wall that girdles the sea-front. In the brilliantly-illuminated restaurants the rich French population gathered about the little tables, while the withered beggars stared in upon the oyster shells, the champagne bottles, and the feathers in the women's audacious hats.

When Mrs. Greyne emerged upon the pavement before the Grand Hotel, attended by Mrs. Forbes and the guide, she paused for a moment, and cast a searching glance upon the fairy scene. In this voluptuous evening and strange environment life seemed oddly dreamlike. She scarcely felt like Mrs. Greyne. Possibly Mrs. Forbes also felt unlike herself, for she suddenly placed one hand upon her left side, and tottered. Abdallah Jack supported her. She screamed aloud.

"Madam!" she said. "It is the vertigo. I am overtook!"

She was really ill; her face, indeed, became the colour of a plover's egg.

"Let me go to bed, madam," she implored. "It is the vertigo, madam. I am overtook!"

Under ordinary circumstances Mrs. Greyne would have prescribed a dose of Kasbah air, but to-night she felt strange, and she wanted strangeness. Mrs. Forbes with the vertigo, in a small carriage, would be inappropriate. She, therefore, bade her retire, mounted into the vehicle with Abdallah Jack, and was quickly driven away, her bonnet strings floating upon the winsome wind.

"You know my husband?" she asked softly of the guide.

Abdallah Jack replied in French that he rather thought he did.

"How is he looking?" continued Mrs. Greyne in a slightly yearning voice. "My Eustace!" she added to herself, "my devoted one!"

"Monsieur Greyne is pale as washed linen upon the Kasbah wall," replied Abdallah Jack, lighting a cigarette, and wreathing the great novelist in its grey-blue smoke. "He is thin as the Spahi's lance, he is nervous as the leaves of the eucalyptus-tree when the winds blow from the north."

Mrs. Greyne was seriously perturbed.

"Would I had come before!" she murmured, with serious self-reproach.

"Monsieur Greyne is worse than all the English," pursued Abdallah Jack in a voice that sounded to Mrs. Greyne decidedly sinister. "He is worse than the tourists of Rook, who laugh in the doorways of the mosques and twine in their hair the dried lizards of the Sahara. Even the guide of Rook rejected him. I only would undertake him because I am full of evil."

Mrs. Greyne began to feel distinctly uncomfortable, and to wish she had not been so ready to pander to Mrs. Forbes' vertigo. She stole a sidelong glance at her strange companion. The carriage was small. The end of his bristling black moustache was very near. What he said of Mr. Greyne did not disturb her, because she knew that her Eustace had sacrificed his reputation to do her service; but what he said about himself was not reassuring.

"I think you must be doing yourself an injustice," she said in a rather agitated voice.

"Madame?"

"I do not believe you are so bad as you imply," she continued.

The carriage turned with a jerk out of the brilliantly-lighted thoroughfare that runs along the sea into a narrow side street, crowded with native Jews, and dark with shadows.

"Madame does not know me."

The exact truth of this observation struck home, like a dagger, to the mind of Mrs. Greyne.

"I am a wicked person," added Abdallah Jack, with a profound conviction. "That is why Monsieur Greyne chose me as his guide."

The novelist began to quake. Her chocolate brocade fluttered. Was she herself to learn at first hand, and on her first evening in Africa, enough about African frailty to last her for the rest of her life? And how much more of life would remain to her after her stock of knowledge had been thus increased? The carriage turned into a second side street, narrower and darker than the last.

"Are we going right?" she said apprehensively.

"No, madame; we are going wrong—we are going to the wicked part of the city."

"But—but—you are sure Mr. Greyne will be there?"

Abdallah Jack laughed sardonically.

"Monsieur Greyne is never anywhere else. Monsieur Greyne is wicked as is a mad Touareg of the desert."

"I don't think you quite understand my husband," said Mrs. Greyne, feeling in duty bound to stand up for her poor, maligned Eustace. "Whatever he may have done he has done at my special request."

"Madame says?"

"I say that in all his proceedings while in Algiers Mr. Greyne has been acting under my directions."

Abdallah Jack fixed his enormous eyes steadily upon her.

"You are his wife, and told him to come here, and to do as he has done?"

"Ye-yes," faltered Mrs. Greyne, for the first time in her life feeling as if she were being escorted towards the criminal dock by a jailer with Puritan tendencies.

"Then it is true what they say on the shores of the great canal," he remarked composedly.

"What do they say?" inquired Mrs. Greyne.

"That England is a land of female devils," returned the guide as the carriage plunged into a filthy alley, between two rows of blind houses, and began to ascend a steep hill.

Mrs. Greyne gasped. She opened her lips to protest vigorously, but her head swam— either from indignation or from fatigue—and she could not utter a word. The horses mounted like cats upward into the dense blackness, from which dropped down the faint sounds of squealing music and of hoarse cries and laughter. The wheels bounded over the stones, sank into the deep ruts, scraped against the sides of the unlighted houses. And Abdallah Jack sat staring at Mrs. Greyne as an English clergyman's wife might stare at the appalling rites of some deadly cannibal encountered in a far-off land, with a stony wonder, a sort of paralysed curiosity.

Suddenly the carriage stopped on a piece of waste land covered with small pebbles. Abdallah Jack sprang out.

"Why do we stop?" said Mrs. Greyne, turning as pale as ashes.

"The carriage can go no farther. Madame must walk."

Mrs. Greyne began to tremble.

"We are to leave the coachman?"

"I shall escort madame, alone."

The great novelist's tongue cleaved to the roof of her mouth. She felt like a Merrin's exercise-book, every leaf of which was covered with African frailty. However, there was no help for it. She had to descend, and stand among the pebbles.

"Where are we going?"

Abdallah Jack waved his hand towards a stone rampart dimly seen in the faint light that emanated from the starry sky.

"Down there into the alley of the Dead Dervishes."

Mrs. Greyne could not repress a cry of horror. At that moment she would have given a thousand pounds to have Mrs. Forbes at her side.

Abdallah Jack grasped her by the hand, and led her ruthlessly forward. Gazing with terror-stricken eyes over the crumbling rampart of the Kasbah, she saw the city far below her, the lights of the streets, the lights of the ships in harbour. She heard the music of a bugle, and wished she were a Zouave safe in barracks. She wished she were a German-Swiss porter, a merry chasseur—anything but Mrs. Eustace Greyne. One thing alone supported her in this hour of trial, the thought of her husband's ecstasy when she appeared upon the dread scene of his awful labours, to tell him that he was released, that he need visit them no more.

The alley of the Dead Dervishes is long and winding. To Mrs. Greyne it seemed endless. As she threaded it with faltering step, gripped by the feverish hand of Abdallah Jack, who now began to display a strange and terrible excitement, she became a centre of curiosity. Unwashed Arabs, rakish Zouaves in blue and red, wandering Jews of various nationalities, unveiled dancing-girls covered with jewels, stared in wonder upon the chocolate brocade and the floating bonnet strings, followed upon her footsteps, pointing with painted fingers, and making remarks of a personal nature in French, Arabic, and other unknown tongues. She moved in the midst of a crowd, on and on before lighted interiors from which wild music flowed.

"Shall we never be there?" she panted to Abdallah Jack. "My limbs refuse their office." She jogged against a Tunisian Jewess in a pointed hat, and rebounded upon an enormous Riff in a tattered sheep-skin. "I can go no farther."

"We are there! Behold the house of the Ouled!"

As he uttered the last word he burst into a bitter laugh, and drew Mrs. Greyne, now gasping for breath, through an open doorway into a little hall of imitation marble, with fluted pillars adorned with oilcloth, and walls hung with imported oleographs. From a chamber on the right, near a winding staircase covered with blue-and-white tiles, came the sound of laughter, of song, and of a hideous music conveyed to the astonied ear by pipes and drums.

"They are in there!" exclaimed Abdallah Jack, folding his arms, and looking at Mrs. Greyne. "Go to your husband!"

Mrs. Greyne put her hands to her magnificent forehead, and tottered forward. She reached the door, she pushed it, she entered. There upon a wooden dais, surrounded by gilt mirrors and artificial roses, she beheld her husband, in a check suit and a white Homburg hat, performing the wildest evolutions, while opposite him a lady, smothered in coloured silks and coins, tattooed and painted, dyed and scented, covered with kohl and crowned with ostrich feathers, screamed a nasal chant of the East, and bounded like an electrified monkey.

"Eustace!" cried Mrs. Greyne, leaning for support against an oleograph.

Her husband turned.

"Eustace!" she cried again. "It is I!"

He stood as if turned to stone. Mrs. Greyne hesitated, started, moved forward to the dais, and stared upon the Ouled, who had also ceased from dancing, and looked strangely surprised, even confused, by the great novelist's intrusion.

"Miss Verbena!" she exclaimed. "Miss Verbena in Algiers!"

"Eugenia!" said Mr. Greyne in a husky voice, "what is this you say? This lady is the Ouled."

A sardonic laugh came from the doorway. They turned. There stood Abdallah Jack. He advanced roughly to the Ouled.

"Come," he said angrily. "Have we not earned the money of the stranger? Have we not earned enough? To-morrow you shall marry me as you have promised, and we will return to our own land, to the canal where you and I were born. And nevermore shall the Levantine instruct the babes of the English devils, but dwell veiled and guarded in the harem of her master."

"Mademoiselle Verbena!" said Mr. Greyne in a more husky voice. "But—but—your dying mother?"

"She sleeps, monsieur, in the white sands of Ismailia, beside the bitter lake. I trust that madame can now go on with the respectable 'Catherine.'"

And with an ironic reverence to Mrs. Eustace Greyne she placed her hand in Abdallah Jack's and vanished from the room.

"Catherine's Repentance," published in a gigantic volume not many weeks ago, was preceded by Mr. Eustace Greyne's. When last heard of he was seated in the magnificent library of the corner house in Park Lane next to the Duke of Ebury's, busily engaged in pasting the newspaper notices of Mrs. Greyne's greatest work into a superb new album.

The Abdallah Jacks have returned to the Suez Canal, bearing with them a snug little fortune to be invested in the purchase of a coal wharf at Port Said, and a remarkably handsome crocodile dressing-case, fitted with gold, and monogrammed with the initials "E. G."

End of the book.